1

Natural Hair and the Law

Tracy Sanders, Esq.

P.O. Box 360764

Los Angeles, CA 90036

info@naturalhairandthelaw.com

Dedication:

I dedicate this book to those who have survived or currently battling hair loss.

I dedicate this book to confident and ubiquitous naturalistas.

Acknowledgments:

To my ancestors, thanks for teaching me to embrace our cultural identity.

To Dwan White, founder of Aunt Jackie's Curls & Coils, thanks for modeling excellence and collaboration.

To Lori Fisher, founder of Best Dooz, thanks for demonstrating innovation and leadership.

Chapter 1 - Introduction

Natural Hair Affirmations is a workbook designed for naturalistas, transitioners, and anyone interested in natural hair topics. The workbook will help you embark upon your natural hair journey with 12 attributes: Divinity, Love, Strength, Transformation, Harmony, Adaptability, Diversity, Intelligence, Energy, Peace, Unity, and Freedom. The purpose of the workbook is to provide a framework for navigating the natural hair journey through a positive mindset. The workbook will help you to track your natural hair progress. The workbook will encourage you to celebrate milestones while reaching your natural hair goals. The workbook provides an overview of laws related to natural hair products and consumer safety.

Here is the agenda for Natural Hair Affirmations:

January – Divinity

February – Love

March – Strength

April – Transformation

May – Harmony

June – Adaptability

July – Diversity

August – Intelligence

September – Energy

October – Peace

November – Unity

December – Freedom

Let us begin and end our natural hair journey this year with positivity!

Chapter 2 – January – Divinity

Sanders Comment:

Begin a new year with the spirit of gratitude! Do not focus on your flaws. Give thanks for everything that is right with you! Namaste.

As I begin a new year, my natural hair goals are:

_____

_____

_____

_____

Avowals:

I am fearfully and wonderfully made!

Chapter 3 – February – Love

Sanders Comment:

Pledge to love your natural hair. Give your hair tender loving care (TLC) through personal care, salon appointments, and scalp massages. If you have a scalp or hair condition, seek medical advice from a dermatologist or trichologist. As you accept and treasure your hair, let love abound forevermore.

I love my natural hair because:

_____

_____

_____

I love my transitioning hair because:

_____

_____

_____

Who taught you to love your natural hair?

_____

_____

_____

Avowals:

Do everything with courage and love.

I will nurture my hair with love.

Love never fails.

Chapter 4 – March – Strength

Sanders Comment:

Similar to a spiritual journey, your natural hair journey requires perseverance and strength. You must have patience if there are set backs or lack of progress. For example, the average for human hair growth is approximately 0.5 inches per month. Perhaps your hair grows at a slower pace. Rather than focusing on length, shift your motivation to healthy hair. Remember to create a healthy hair care regimen, which promotes optimal functioning of your scalp.

As a naturalista, you may need discipline, strength, and courage to be yourself.

If you are in a restrictive work environment, it may take self-confidence to balance cultural

identity and employment because: _____

_____

In a romantic relationship, you may have to comprise natural hair or natural hairstyles if _____

_____

In some instances, a naturalista must be unapologetically _____

Avowals:

The body may be weak but God is my strength.

My hair is healthy and strong.

I am capable, powerful, and strong!

Chapter 5 – April – Transformation

Sanders Comment:

The need for a positive mindset is due in part to the negative messages imposed upon African descent people from around the world. Kinky/curly hair appears to be denigrated in society, media, institutions, and even in some families. The natural hair community is a refreshing change in our psyche as a community. We are boldly saying to the world - I have kinky/curly hair. I am fierce, fabulous, and beautiful.

Returning to natural hair made me feel:

_____

_____

_____

Natural hair is your hair texture at birth. How would you define natural hair?

_____

_____

_____

Natural hair may necessitate a commitment to change your lifestyle (T/F).

How did you survive the natural hair transition?

_____

_____

_____

Did you change your healthy hair care regimen?

_____

_____

_____

Do you think the natural hair movement is promoting economic empowerment of African descent people?

_____

_____

_____

The natural hair community is global. (T/F)

Do you think the natural hair movement provides an opportunity for global change and international dialogue?

_____

_____

_____

Avowals:

Transformation begins with a positive mindset.

I am changing for the betterment of humanity.

I am transforming into someone with healthier hair.

Chapter 6 – May – Harmony

Sanders Comment:

Enjoy the sweetness of life with your "curl" friends. Sing a tune as you massage your scalp! Listen to your favorite song as you get through "wash day!" Happiness and a positive mindset may affect the physiology of your scalp and hair. Combined with regular TLC, this may help reverse damage or promote new growth!

I enjoy spending time with my "curl" friends. We share natural hair tips and natural hair product samples.

How many "curl" friends do you have to support your natural hair journey? _____

Did you join a natural hair meet up? _____

Have you considered membership in a natural hair meetup?

_____

_____

_____

_____

Did you attend a natural hair event? If so, what did you learn?

_____

_____

_____

_____

How do you learn about the latest trends for natural hair or natural hairstyles?

_____

_____

_____

_____

Which natural hair product brands and influencers do you follow?

_____

_____

_____

_____

Avowals:

I am in harmony with myself and my "curl" friends!

Taking care of my hair is something that I do on "wash day" and every day.

My hair is beautiful!

Chapter 7 – June – Adaptability

Sanders Comment:

Nothing remains constant except change itself. In addition, this is truth in all of our lives. Change is inevitable. Regardless of the situation, remember to take care of your hair.

Congrats! You have reached the midpoint of this year! You have achieved a milestone in your natural hair journey! How do you feel?

_____

_____

_____

_____

Do you notice any emotional, mental, physical, or spiritual changes?

_____

_____

_____

_____

Do you have an action plan for the remainder of this year?

_____

_____

_____

_____

Avowals:

I wear protective hairstyles and adapt to changes in the weather.

I can adapt to changes in my hair as a transitioner.

My hair is recovering from damage and growing back naturally.

Chapter 8 – July – Diversity

Sanders Comment:

Do not touch my hair! That is what we want to say when others ask to do so. Perhaps it is an inquiry based on adoration. There is beauty in diversity.

The three human hair textures are straight, curly, and kinky.

What is your natural hair texture? _____

_____

_____

What are alternatives to "good hair" or "bad hair" as metaphors for genetic variances in human hair

textures? _____

_____

_____

Do you think there is discrimination at work or in the schools based on appearance? _____

_____

_____

Have you ever treated another person unfairly based on appearance? _____

_____

_____

Some ways to respect others from various cultural, racial, and socio-economic backgrounds are: _____

_____

_____

Natural hair discrimination in the workplace is illegal (T/F)

See Title VII of the Civil Rights Act of 1964

An employer may ban natural hairstyles in the workplace such as cornrows, braids, and dreadlocks. (T/F)

See <u>EEOC v. Catastrophe Management Solutions</u>, No. 14-13482 (11th Cir. Sept. 15, 2016)

Natural hair discrimination in the schools is illegal. (T/F)

See Title VI of the Civil Rights of 1964

Avowals:

I am in favor of diversity in the natural hair community.

My hair is unique!

Others may want to touch my hair because it is amazing!

Chapter 9 – August – Intelligence

Sanders Comment:

We have heard that knowledge is power. This epithet resonates loudly in the natural hair community. Fortunately, there is a wealth of knowledge about natural hair care available online, in hair salons, and by attending natural hair care events. Some social media influencers have a significant amount of followers who appreciate valuable natural hair tips. However, your primary resource may be a natural hair care specialist. If you have hair loss due to a medical condition, you may rely on your medical provider. Do not forget that natural hair is a living part of your human body. Natural hair may be enhanced through science advancement.

According to Mintel, a marketing research firm, the natural hair care industry is expansive and worth multi-millions.

There are wide varieties of natural hair product brands. What are your favorite natural hair product brands?

1. _____

2. _____

3. _____

Where do you buy natural hair products?

a) Stores
b) Online
c) Salons
d) Expos

Do you purchase organic natural hair care products? _____

Do you read labels before purchasing natural hair care products? _____

Overview of Food and Drug Law:

It is important to determine if hair products are labeled accurately and safe for consumers in the marketplace.

The Food and Drug Administration (FDA) regulates cosmetics in the United States.

According to the FDA, cosmetics include products, except soap, applied for cleansing, beautifying, or altering appearance.

Examples of cosmetics are makeup, fragrances, and hair products.

The FDA enforces two acts to protect consumers from unsafe, mislabeled, or misbranded cosmetics:

(1) Fair Packaging and Labeling Act (FP&L) - See 15 U.S.C. 1451 – 1460

(2) Food, Drug, and Cosmetic Act of 1938 (FD&C Act) – See 21 U.S.C. 321-392.

The FD&C Act protects consumers from unsafe or fraudulent labeling practices.

The FD&C Act prohibits marketing of misbranded labels.

Since the FDA classifies hair products as cosmetics, labels cannot be:

- Misbranded (false or misleading labels)
- Mislabeled (labels must state an accurate name and address of the manufacturer, packer, or distributor)
- Hidden (labels must have terms that are easy to read and understand)
- Deceptive (accurate container and net quantity of contents).

See Sec. 602, FD&C Act

Are you concerned about natural hair products being misbranded or mislabeled?

_____

_____

_____

_____

What can we do in the natural hair community to promote consumer safety in the natural hair care industry?

_____

_____

_____

_____

Do you make your own natural hair products?

_____

_____

_____

Now let us discuss your healthy hair care regimen in the salon or at home!

_____'s Healthy Hair Care Regimen

Do you know how to build a good healthy hair care regimen? _____

First, _____

Second, _____

Third, _____

Fourth, _____

Remember to take care of for your scalp and hair. Your scalp and hair may require different natural hair products. Follow the instructions for all hair products carefully.

Overuse or misuse of hair products may inhibit growth and cause hair loss. (T/F)

Did you ever have a bad experience with any hair product brands? _____

_____

Did you report an adverse event to a natural hair product company? _____

_____

Natural Hair Education Questionnaire:

How often do you visit a hair salon? _____

_____

Do you have a regularly scheduled "wash day" at home? _____

_____

Do you co-wash or pre-poo? _____

_____

What is your favorite shampoo or cleanser? _____

_____

Do you have a scalp or hair condition that requires a medicated shampoo or cleanser? _____

_____

Sleeping on a pillowcase with residue from hair products could cause acne breakouts. (T/F)

What is your favorite conditioner? _____

_____

What is your favorite deep conditioner? _____

_____

How often do you deep condition your hair? _____

_____

Do you have a heated conditioning cap? _____

_____

Do you use a detangling product? _____

_____

Do you prefer detangling with your fingers, comb, or hairbrush? _____

_____

It is important to wash your hands after using natural hair products because residue could be under your fingernails. (T/F)

What is your favorite moisturizer? _____

_____

Do you use hair oil? If so, what are your favorite hair oils? _____

_____

What are your favorite hair styling products? _____

_____

_____

Do you wear natural hair extensions, clips, or wigs? _____

_____

_____

How often do you "trim" your ends? _____

_____

_____

Do you prefer to have your natural hair specialist "trim" your ends?

_____

_____

_____

_____

What are the best foods for healthy hair?

_____

_____

_____

_____

What are the best vitamins for healthy hair?

_____

_____

_____

_____

What are the best minerals for healthy hair?

_____

_____

_____

_____

What can you do to ensure that nutrition and oxygen are flowing to your scalp?

_____

_____

_____

_____

Do you watch natural hair care video tutorials for natural hair grooming tips?

_____

_____

_____

_____

Do you read natural hair care books, magazines, articles, or blog postings?

_____

_____

_____

_____

Did you discuss your healthy hair care regimen with a hair stylist?

_____

_____

_____

How do you measure healthy hair growth? _____

_____

_____

_____

How do you monitor healthy hair growth? _____

_____

_____

_____

How do you feel when achieving desired outcomes? _____

_____

_____

_____

Do you share your healthy hair care successes to help others? _____

_____

_____

_____

Do you share your healthy hair care failures to help others? _____

_____

_____

_____

Avowals:

I am in control of my healthy hair care regimen.

My hair, skin, and nails reflect good health and hygiene!

Knowledge is power!

Chapter 10 – September – Energy

Sanders Comment:

Positive energy will help you focus during your natural hair journey. Relax and allow your blood vessels to provide nutrients to your hair bulbs. Write the vision and make it plain – your hair is stronger with more vitality!

Energy may be defined as spirit, life, and vitality.

In some cultures and religious beliefs, hair has a connection to energy.

How would you define your cultural identity? _____

How would you define your religious belief? _____

What are your cultural beliefs about hair?

- Spirit _____

- Life _____

- Vitality _____

What are your religious beliefs about hair?

- Spirit _____

- Life _____

- Vitality _____

Hair Science:

The components of hair are:

(1) Hair Shaft (visible above the skin)

(2) Keratin (protein)

(3) Follicle (anchor)

(4) Hair Bulb (base)

(5) Blood Vessels (transport nutrients)

(6) Hormones (modification of hair based on life stage)

Hair growth consists of three phases:

(1) Anagen (growth)
(2) Catagen (transitional)
(3) Telogen (resting)

What is your current phase of hair growth? _____

The pigment in hair cells determines natural hair color.

What is your natural hair color? _____

What is your current hair color? _____

Do you think naturalistas should use chemicals to change their hair color? _____

_____

_____

As pigment cells die, hair turns grey. Do you have gray hair? _____

If yes, what age did you begin to notice gray hair? _____

Noticing gray hair on my head made me feel: _____

_____

_____

Did you apply chemicals to change the color of your gray hair? _____

_____

_____

If you have gray hair, it is a symbol of: _____

_____

_____

Why is it important for intergenerational naturalistas to share hair stories? _____

_____

_____

Comment below how each generation may contribute to the natural hair community.

Silent Generation: _____

Baby Boomer: _____

Generation X:_____

Millennial:_____

If you do not have gray hair, how do you feel about "turning" gray hair in the future?

_____

_____

_____

Avowals:

I think good thoughts to send positive energy to my hair!

My blood vessels provide nourishment to my hair cells and follicles.

I can adjust to hormonal changes that may affect my hair.

Chapter 11 – October – Peace

Sanders Comment:

I have peace of mind about my hair. I am not anxious about how others perceive me. In every situation, I am grateful for the opportunity to learn more about others and myself.

Suffering from hair loss can be a devastating experience.

Survivors who are currently battling hair loss may need encouragement and support.

In some instances, hair loss results from an underlying medical condition.

Coping with hair loss and an underlying medical condition might be a test of endurance.

What are some effective coping mechanisms? _____

_____

_____

If you are a survivor of hair loss, how can you help others? _____

_____

_____

Which hair products do you think are effective for treating hair loss? _____

_____

_____

Do you wear wigs or hairpieces because of hair loss? _____

_____

_____

If you are currently battling hair loss, did you research herbal or natural remedies? _____

_____

_____

What is the best way to find a hair stylist to treat hair loss? _____

_____

_____

Did you seek a mental health counselor or support group to cope with hair loss?

_____

_____

_____

Surviving or battling hair loss has taught me:

_____

_____

_____

Avowals:

My scalp is in good health.

My hair is growing.

I am a survivor!

Chapter 12 – November – Unity

Sanders Comment:

I am an advocate for unity in the natural hair community. Do not make assumptions based on appearance. Every naturalista has good and bad hair days. Build bridges with your fellow "curl" mates not walls.

What is your vision of naturally beautiful hair?

_____

_____

_____

How would you describe your natural hair?

_____

_____

_____

What is "monoracial" hair? _____

_____

_____

What is "multicultural hair"? _____

_____

_____

What is your natural hair type? Commonly used descriptions are posted below.

   a) 3A (Loopy curls)
   b) 3B (Defined curls)
   c) 3C (Corkscrew curls)
   d) 4A (S shape curls)
   e) 4B (Z shape curls)
   f) 4C (Coily curls)

What kind of natural hair products are best for your hair type? _____

_____

_____

When I see my natural hair in the mirror, I feel:

_____

_____

_____

In the past, I have compared my natural hair to another person's such as:

a) Grandmother
b) Mother
c) Sister
d) Cousin
e) Spouse
f) Friend
g) Co-worker
h) None of the above

In the present, I do/do not measure my natural hair by society's standard of beauty.

If you measure your natural hair by society's standard of beauty, how does this make you feel?

_____

_____

_____

Of the four attributes below, which one could be further developed to overcome negative emotions about your natural hair?

a) Self-acceptance
b) Self-awareness
c) Self-esteem
d) Self-trust

While attending natural hair events, I feel connected to the natural hair community because:

_____

_____

_____

Do you think there is division in the natural hair community based on various hair types?

_____

_____

_____

What can we do in the natural hair community to promote unity and focus on commonality regardless of hair types?

_____

_____

_____

Avowals:

I am empowered and promote unity among all hair types!

My hair is not defined by another person's crown and glory.

I am proud of my hair!

Chapter 13 – December – Freedom

Sanders Comment:

There is freedom in being your authentic self. Naturalistas are champions of natural hair freedom! Do not become discouraged because of the recent cases about natural hair in the workplace and schools. Some dress and grooming codes may have an adverse impact on employment and education opportunities for people of African descent with kinky/curly hair. International organizations should collaborate to protect the rights of naturalistas around the world.

Returning to natural hair means I am no longer in bondage to:

1. _____

2. _____

3. _____

4.

   _____

5. _____

6. _____

7. _____

If you are a transitioner, the adjustment might be challenging because:

_____

_____

_____

Do you think it is fair to judge others or make negative remarks about their hair status (natural, transitioner, or chemical treatment)?

_____

_____

_____

Do you encourage others who are making the transition back to natural hair?

_____

_____

_____

Naturalistas Are Swimming Champions!

As a swimmer, the pros of natural hair are:

(1)

(2)

(3)

(4)

(5)

What are some ways to prevent hair damage before swimming in a pool or at the beach?

_____

_____

_____

As a swimmer, the cons of natural hair are:

(1)

(2)

(3)

(4)

(5)

What are some ways to prevent hair damage after swimming in a pool or at the beach?

_____

_____

_____

What are the best natural hair products for naturalistas who swim?

_____

_____

_____

Avowals:

My hair is alive, vibrant, and free!

Each day my scalp and hair become healthier.

I let go of pressure to conform my natural hair.

Chapter 14 – Summary

Reflect upon your natural hair journey from beginning until the end of this year. Did you achieve your natural hair goals? Did you experience personal growth? Did you experience professional growth?

_____

_____

_____

_____

What are your natural hair goals for next year?

_____

_____

_____

_____

How could others benefit from your natural hair journey?

_____

_____

_____

_____

The best way to fight an alien and oppressive culture is to value your own.

Answer Key

True/False:

All statements are (T) True.

Fill In the Blank:

Please use your personal experience to complete this section of the workbook.

Overview of Food and Drug Law:

Examples of cosmetics are makeup, fragrances, and hair products.

The FDA enforces two acts to protect consumers from unsafe, mislabeled, or misbranded cosmetics:

(1) Fair Packaging and Labeling Act (FP&L) - See 15 U.S.C. 1451 – 1460

(2) Food, Drug, and Cosmetic Act of 1938 (FD&C Act) – See 21 U.S.C. 321-392.

The FD&C Act protects consumers from unsafe or fraudulent labeling practices.

The FD&C Act prohibits marketing of misbranded labels.

Since the FDA classifies hair products as cosmetics, labels cannot be:

- Misbranded (false or misleading labels)
- Mislabeled (labels must state an accurate name and address of the manufacturer, packer, or distributor)
- Hidden (labels must have terms that are easy to read and understand)
- Deceptive (accurate container and net quantity of contents).

See Sec. 602, FD&C Act

Notes

Biography

Tracy Sanders is an attorney, author, and speaker in Los Angeles, CA. She is founder of Natural Hair and the Law, (www.naturalhairandthelaw.com), which is an organization formed to provide publications, workshops, and events addressing legal issues related to natural hair in the workplace and schools. She earned a Juris Doctor at Syracuse University College of Law in 2002, Master of Public Administration at the University of South Carolina in 1998, and Bachelor of Arts in Political Science at the University of South Carolina in 1995. Tracy enjoys yoga, traveling, and community service. She is particularly interested in community service initiatives to help young people achieve their education and career goals. Tracy has made appearances on networks such as ABC, FOX, MSNBC, TLC, and WE.

Natural Hair and the Law
Tracy Sanders, Esq.

Made in the USA
Las Vegas, NV
08 January 2021